'With one's face in the wind you were almost burned with a shower of Firedrops . . .'

SAMUEL PEPYS
Born 1633, London
Died 1703, Clapham

PEPYS IN PENGUIN CLASSICS
The Diary of Samuel Pepys

SAMUEL PEPYS

The Great Fire of London

PENGUIN BOOKS

PENGUIN CLASSICS

Published by the Penguin Group
Penguin Books Ltd, 80 Strand, London wc2r orl, England
Penguin Group (USA) Inc., 375 Hudson Street, New York, New York 10014, USA
Penguin Group (Canada), 90 Eglinton Avenue East, Suite 700, Toronto, Ontario,
Canada m4p 2y3 (a division of Pearson Penguin Canada Inc.)
Penguin Ireland, 25 St Stephen's Green, Dublin 2, Ireland
(a division of Penguin Books Ltd)
Penguin Group (Australia), 707 Collins Street, Melbourne, Victoria 3008, Australia
(a division of Pearson Australia Group Pty Ltd)
Penguin Books India Pvt Ltd, 11 Community Centre, Panchsheel Park,
New Delhi – 110 017, India
Penguin Group (NZ), 67 Apollo Drive, Rosedale, Auckland 0632, New Zealand
(a division of Pearson New Zealand Ltd)
Penguin Books (South Africa) (Pty) Ltd, Block D, Rosebank Office Park,
181 Jan Smuts Avenue, Parktown North, Gauteng 2193, South Africa

Penguin Books Ltd, Registered Offices: 80 Strand, London wc2r orl, England

www.penguin.com

This selection published in Penguin Classics 2015
002

Set in 9.5/13 pt Baskerville 10 Pro
Typeset by Jouve (UK), Milton Keynes
Printed in Great Britain by Clays Ltd, St Ives plc

A CIP catalogue record for this book is available from the British Library

isbn: 978–0–141–39754–2

www.greenpenguin.co.uk

Contents

During this period Pepys is Clerk of the Acts to the Navy Board and concerned with the ultimately abortive English colony of 'Tanger' (Tangier), part of Catherine of Braganza's dowry (together with Bombay) when she married the now reigning monarch Charles II. Pepys is also engaged more broadly with the management of the Royal Navy which is fighting what proved to be the unsuccessful Second Anglo-Dutch War. Much of the first extract is concerned both with the spread of the Plague and with the prosecution of the war. The news of the English victory off Lowestoft is described, with the fleet commanded by Charles II's younger brother the Duke of York (later James II). The second extract describes the Great Fire of London. Throughout the text Pepys refers to personal friends and family, scientific colleagues and naval colleagues. The Duke of Albemarle (the former George Monck) is Captain-General. The Earl of Sandwich ('My Lord') is Pepys' patron. 'Mr Evelings' is the diarist John Evelyn.

May 1665

1. Up, and to Mr Povy's, and by his bedside talked a good while. Thence to the Duke of Albemarle, where I sorry to find myself to come a little late. And so home, and at noon, going to the Change, met my Lord Brunkerd, Sir Robert Murry, Deane Wilkins, and Mr Hooke, going by coach to Coll. Blunt's to dinner. So they stopped and took me with them. Landed at the Tower wharf and thence by water to Greenwich, and there coaches met us and to his house, a very stately seat for situation and brave plantations; and among others, a Vineyard. No extraordinary dinner, nor any other entertainment good – but only, after dinner to the tryall of some experiments about making of coaches easy. And several we tried, but one did prove mighty easy (not here for me to describe, but the whole body of that coach lies upon one long spring) and we all, one after another, rid in it; and it is very fine and likely to take. These experiments were the intent of their coming, and pretty they are. Thence back by coach to Greenwich and in his pleasure-boat to Deptford; and there stopped, and in to Mr Evelings, which is a most

beautiful place, but it being dark and late, I stayed not; but Dean Wilkins and Mr Hooke and I walked to Redriffe, and noble discourse all day long did please me. And it being late, did take them to my house to drink, and did give them some sweetmeats – and thence sent them with a lanthorn home – two worthy persons as are in England, I think, or the world. So to my Lady Batten, where my wife is tonight; and so after some merry talk, home to bed.

3. Up betimes, and walked to Sir Ph. Warwickes, where a long time with him in his chamber alone, talking of Sir G. Carteret's business and the abuses he puts on the nation by his bad payments – to both our vexations; but no hope of remedy for aught I see. So to the Change and thence home to dinner; and so out to Gresham College and saw a cat killed with the Duke of Florence's poison. And saw it proved that the oyle of Tobacco, drawn by one of the Society, doth the same effect, and is judged to be the same thing with the poison, both in colour and smell and effect. (I saw also an abortive child, preserved fresh in spirit of salt). Thence parted, and to Whitehall to the council chamber about an order touching the Navy (our being impowered to commit seamen or maisters that do not, being hired or pressed, fallow their work), but they could give us none. So, a little vexed at that, because I put in the memorial to the Duke of Albemarle alone,

under my own hand – home; and after some time at the office, home to bed.

5. Up betimes, and by water to Westminster, there to speak the first time with Sir Robt. Long, to give him my privy seal and my Lord Treasurers order for Tanger Tallys. He received me kindly enough. Thence home by water; and presently down to Woolwige and back to Blackewall, and there viewed the Breach, in order to a mast-Docke; and so to Deptford to the Globe, where my Lord Brunkard, Sir J. Mennes, Sir W. Batten, and Comissioner Pett were at dinner, having been at the Breach also – but they find it will be of too great charge to make use of it. After dinner to Mr Evelings; he being abroad, we walked in his garden, and a lovely noble ground he hath endeed. And among other rarities, a hive of Bees; so, as being hived in glass, you may see the Bees making their honey and Combs mighty pleasantly. Thence home, and I by and by to Mr Povy's to see him, who is yet in his chamber, not well. And thence by his advice to one Lovetts, a Varnisher, to see his manner of new varnish, but found not him at home; but his wife a very beautiful woman, who showed me much variety of admirable work; and is in order to my having of some papers fitted with lines, for my use for Tables and the like. I know not whether I was more pleased with the thing, or that I was showed it by her. But resolved I am to have some made.

So home to my office late, and then to supper and to bed. My wife tells me that she hears that my poor aunt James hath had her breast cut off here in town – her breast having long been out of order. This day, after I had suffered my own hayre to grow long, in order to wearing it, I find the convenience of Perrywiggs is so great, that I have cut off all short again, and will keep to periwigs.

7. *Lords day*. Up, and to church with my wife. Home and dined. After dinner came Mr Andrews, and spent the afternoon with me about our Tanger business of the victuals and then parted. And after sermon comes Mr Hill and a gentleman, a friend of his, one Mr Scott, that sings well also; and then comes Mr Andrews, and we all sung and supped; and then to sing again, and passed the Sunday very pleasantly and soberly; and so I to my office a little, and then home to prayers and to bed. Yesterday begun my wife to learn to Limb of one Browne, which Mr Hill helps her to. And by her beginning, upon some eyes, I think she will [do] very fine things – and I shall take great delight in it.

9. Up betimes, and to my business at the office, where all the morning. At noon comes Mrs The[oph]. Turner and dines with us. And my wife's painting-maister stayed and dined, and I take great pleasure in thinking that my wife will really come to something in that business. Here

dined also Luellin. So after dinner to the office and there very busy till almost midnight, and so home to supper and to bed. This day we have news of eight ships being taken by some of ours, going into the Texell, their two men of war that convoyed [them] running in. They came from about Ireland, round to the North.

10.   Up betimes, and abroad to the Cockepitt, where the Duke[1] did give Sir W. Batten and me an account of the late taking of eight ships and of his[2] intent to come back to the Gunfleete with the fleet presently – which creates us much work and haste therein, against the fleet comes. So to Mr Povy; and after discourse with him, home and thence to the Guard in Southworke, there to get some soldiers, by the Duke's order, to go keep press-men on board our ships. So to the Change and did much business; and then home to dinner and there find my poor mother come out of the country today, in good health; and I am glad to see her, but my business, which I am sorry for, keeps me from paying the respect I ought to her at her first coming – she being grown very weak in her judgment, and doting again in her discourse, through age and some trouble in her family. Left her and my wife to go abroad to buy something, and then I to my office.

1.   Albemarle.
2.   The Duke of York's.

In the evening, by appointment to Sir W. Warren and Mr Dering at a tavern hard by, with intent to do some good upon their agreement in a great bargain of plank. So home to my office again, and then to supper and to bed, my mother being in bed already.

12.   By water to the Exchequer, and there up and down through all the offices to strike my tallies for 17500*l* – which methinks is so great a testimony of the goodness of God to me; that I, from a mean clerk there, should come to strike tallies myself for that sum, and in the authority that I do now, is a very stupendous mercy to me. I shall have them struck tomorrow. But to see how every little fellow looks after his fees, and to get what he can for everything, is a strange consideration – the King's Fees, that he must pay himself for this 17500*l*, coming to above 100*l*. Thence, called my wife at Unthankes, to the New Exchange and elsewhere to buy a lace band for me, but we did not buy. But I find it so necessary to have some handsome clothes, that I cannot but lay out some money there-upon.

13.   Up, and all day in some little grutchings of pain, as I use to have – from Winde – arising, I think, from my fasting so long and want of exercise – and I think, going so hot in clothes, the weather being hot and I in the same clothes I wore all winter. To the Change after office, and received my Wach from the watchmaker; and a very fine

[one] it is – given me by Briggs the Scrivener. But Lord, to see how much of my old folly and childishnesse hangs upon me still, that I cannot forbear carrying my watch in my hand in the coach all this afternoon, and seeing what a-clock it is 100 times. And am apt to think with myself: how could I be so long without one – though I remember since, I had one and found it a trouble, and resolved to carry one no more about me while I lived.

14. *Lords day*. Up, and with my wife to church, it being Whitsunday. My wife very fine in a new yellow birds-eye Hood, as the fashion is now. We had a most sorry sermon. So home to dinner, my mother having her new suit brought home, which makes her very fine. After dinner my wife and she and Mercer to Tho. Pepys's wife's christening of his first child. And I took a coach and to Wanstead, the house where Sir H. Mildmay did [live] and now Sir Rob. Brookes lives, having bought it of the Duke of Yorke, it being forfeited to him. A fine seat, but an old-fashion house and being not full of people, looks desolately. Thence to Walthamstow, where Sir W. Batten by and by came home, I walking up and down the house and garden with my Lady, very pleasant. Then to supper, very merry; and then back by coach by dark night – I, all the afternoon in the coach, reading the treasonous book of the Court of King James, printed a great while ago and worth reading, though ill intended. As soon as came

home, upon a letter from Duke of Albemarle, I took boat, at about 12 at night, and down the River in a galley, my boy and I, down to the Hope, and so up again, sleeping and waking with great pleasure; my business, to call upon every one of our victualling ships to set them a-going.

15.   And so home; and after dinner, to the King's playhouse all alone, and saw *Loves Maistresse*. Some pretty things and good variety in it, but no or little fancy in it. Thence to the Duke of Albemarle to give him account of my day's works – where he showed me letters from Sir G. Downing, of four days' date, that the Duch are come out and joyned – well-manned and resolved to board our best ships; and fight for certain they will. Thence to the Swan at Herberts, and there the company of Sarah a little while; and so away and called at the Harp and Ball, where the maid, Mary, is very formosa; but Lord, to see in what readiness I am, upon the expiring of my vowes this day, to begin to run into all my pleasures and neglect of business. Thence home; and being sleepy, to bed.

22.   Up, and down to the ships, which now are hindered from going to the fleet (to our great sorrow and shame) with the provisions, the wind being against them. So to the Duke of Albemarle – and thence down by water to Deptford, it being Trinity Monday and so the day of choosing the Master of Trinity house for the next year – where, to my great content, I find that contrary to the

practice and design of Sir W. Batten to break the rule and custom of the Company in choosing their Masters by succession, he would have brought in Sir W. Rider or Sir W. Pen over the head of Hurleston (who is a knave too besides, I believe): the Younger Brothers did all oppose it against the Elder, and with great heat did carry it for Hurleston – which I know will vex him to the heart. Thence, the election being over, to church; where an idle sermon from that conceited fellow Dr Britton, saving that his advice to unity and laying aside all envy and enmity among them was very apposite. Thence walked to Redriffe, and so to the Trinity house; and a great dinner, as is usual. And so to my office, where busy all the afternoon till late; and then home to bed – being much troubled in mind for several things. First, for the condition of the fleet for lack of provisions. The blame this office lies under, and the shame that they deserve to have brought upon them for the ships not being gone out of the River. And then for my business of Tanger, which is not settled; and lastly, for fear that I am not observed to have attended the office business of late as much as I ought to do, though there hath been nothing but my attendance on Tanger that hath occasioned my absence, and that of late not much.

24. Up by 4 a-clock in the morning; and with W. Hewer there till 12 without intermission, putting some papers in order. Thence to the coffee-house with Creed, where I

have not been a great while – where all the news is of the Dutch being gone out – and of the plague growing upon us in this town and of remedies against it; some saying one thing, some another.

28. *Lords day.* Went to chapel and heard a little Musique and there met with Creed, and with him a little while walking and to Wilkinsons for me to drink, being troubled with Winde; and at noon to Sir Ph. Warwicke's to dinner, where abundance of company came in unexpectedly. And here I saw one pretty piece of household stuff; as the company encreaseth, to put a larger leaf upon an Ovall table. After dinner much good discourse with Sir Phillip, who I find, I think, a most pious good man, and a professor of a philosiphicall manner of life and principles like Epictetus, whom he cites in many things. Thence to my Lady Sandwiches, where to my shame I had not been a great while before. Here, upon my telling her a story of my Lord of Rochester's running away on Friday night last with Mrs Mallet, the great beauty and fortune of the [West], who had supped at Whitehall with Mrs Stewart and was going home to her lodgings with her grandfather, my Lord Haly, by coach, and was at Charing cross seized on by both horse- and foot-men and forcibly taken from him, and put into a coach with six horses and two women provided to receive her, and carried away. Upon immediate pursuit, my Lord of Rochester (for whom the King had spoke to the lady often, but with

no success) was taken at Uxbridge; but the lady is not yet heard of, and the King mighty angry and the Lord sent to the Tower. Hereupon, my Lady did confess to me, as a great secret, her being concerned in this story – for if this match breaks between my Lord Rochester and her, then, by the consent of all her friends, my Lord Hinchingbrooke stands fair, and is invited for her. She is worth, and will be at her mother's death (who keeps but a little from her), 2500*l* per annum. Pray God give a good success to it. But my poor Lady, who is afeared of the sickness and resolved to be gone into the country, is forced to stay in town a day or two or three about it, to see the event of it. Thence home, and to see my Lady Pen – where my wife and I were shown a fine rarity: of fishes kept in a glass of water, that will live so for ever; and finely marked they are, being foreign. So to supper at home and to bed.

29. Lay long in bed, being in some little pain of the wind, Collique. Then up and to the Duke of Albemarle, and so to the Swan and there drank at Herberts; and so by coach home, it being kept a great holiday through the City, for the birth and restoration of the King. To my office, where I stood by and saw Symson the Joyner do several things, little Jobbs, to the rendering of my closet handsome and the setting up of some neat plats that Burston hath for my money made me. And so home to dinner; and then, with my wife, mother, and Mercer in one boat, and I in another, down to Woolwich, I walking

from Greenwich, the others going to and fro upon the water till my coming back, having done but little business. So home and to supper, and weary to bed. We have everywhere taken some prizes. Our merchants have good luck to come home safe: Colliers from the North, and some Streights-men just now – and our Hambrough ships, of whom we were so much afeared, are safe in Hambrough. Our Fleete resolved to sail out again from Harwich in a day or two.

June 1665

1.   Up, and to the office, where sat all the morning. At noon to the Change and there did some business and home to dinner, whither Creed comes. And after dinner I put on my new silk Camelott Sute, the best that ever I wore in my life, the suit costing me above 24*l*. In this I went with him to Goldsmiths hall to the burial of Sir Tho. Viner; which hall, and Haberdashers also, was so full of people, that we were fain for ease and coolness to go forth to Paternoster row to choose a silk to make me a plain ordinary suit. That done, we walked to Cornehill, and there at Mr Cades stood in the Balcon and saw all the funerals, which was with the Bluecoat boys and old men – all the Aldermen, and Lord Mayor, &c., and the number of the company very great – the greatest I ever did see for a Taverne. Hither came up to us Dr Allen – and then Mr Povy and Mr Fox. The show being over, and my discourse with Mr Povy – I took coach and to Westminster hall, where I took the fairest flower and by coach to Tothill fields for the ayre, till it was dark. I light, and in with the fairest flower to eat a cake, and there did do as

much as was safe with my flower, and that was enough on my part. Broke up, and away without any notice; and after delivering the rose where it should be, I to the Temple and light; and came to the middle door and there took another coach, and so home – to write letters; but very few, God knows, being (by my pleasure) made to forget everything that is. The coachman that carried [us] cannot know me again, nor the people at the house where we were. Home to bed, certain news being come that our fleet is in sight of the Dutch ships.

2.   Met an express from Sir W. Batten at Harwich, that the fleet is all sailed from Solebay, having spied the Dutch Fleete at sea – and that if the Calmes hinder not, they must needs be now engaged with them.

3.   All this day, by all people upon the River and almost everywhere else hereabout, were heard the Guns, our two fleets for certain being engaged; which was confirmed by letters from Harwich, but nothing perticular; and all our hearts full of concernment for the Duke, and I perticularly for my Lord Sandwich and Mr Coventry after his Royal Highness.

7.   This day, much against my Will, I did in Drury lane see two or three houses marked with a red cross upon the doors, and 'Lord have mercy upon us' writ there – which was a sad sight to me, being the first of that kind that to

my remembrance I ever saw. It put me into an ill concep-
tion of myself and my smell, so that I was forced to buy
some roll tobacco to smell to and chaw – which took away
the apprehension.

8.   About 5 a-clock my wife came home, it having light-
ened all night hard, and one great shower of rain. She
came and lay upon the bed. I up, and to the office, where
all the morning. I alone at home to dinner, my wife, mother,
and Mercer dining at W. Joyces, I giving her a caution to
go round by the Half Moone to his house, because of the
plague. I to my Lord Treasurer's, by appointment of Sir
Tho. Ingram's, to meet the goldsmiths – where I met with
the great news, at last newly come, brought by Bab May
from the Duke of Yorke, that we have totally routed the
Dutch. That the Duke himself, the Prince, my Lord Sandwich, and Mr Coventry are all well. Which did put me
into such a joy, that I forgot almost all other thoughts.
The sum of the news is:

Victory over the Dutch. June. 3. 1665.

This day they engaged – the Dutch neglecting greatly
the opportunity of the wind they had of us – by which
they lost the benefit of their fireships. The Earl of Fal-
mouth, Muskery, and Mr Rd. Boyle killed on board the
Dukes ship, the *Royall Charles*, with one shot. Their blood
and brains flying in the Duke's face – and the head of
Mr Boyle striking down the Duke, as some say. Earle of

Marlbrough, Portland, Rere-[A]dm. Sansum (to Prince Rupert) killed, and Capt. Kirby and Ableson. Sir Jo. Lawson wounded on the knee – hath had some bones taken out, and is likely to be well again. Upon receiving the hurt, he sent to the Duke for another to command the *Royall Oake*. The Duke sent Jordan out of the *St George*, who did brave things in her. Capt. Jer. Smith of the *Mary* was second to the Duke, and stepped between him and Capt. Seaton of the *Urania* (76 guns and 400 men), who had sworn to board the Duke. Killed him, 200 men, and took the ship. Himself losing 99 men, and never an officer saved but himself and Lieutenant. His maister endeed is saved, with his leg cut off. Adm. Opdam blown up. Trump killed, and said by Holmes. All the rest of their Admiralls, as they say, but Everson (whom they dare not trust for his affection to the prince of Orange) are killed. We have taken and sunk, as is believed, about 24 of their best ships. Killed and taken near 8 or 10000 men; and lost, we think, not above 700. A great victory, never known in the world. They are all fled; some 43 got into the Texell and others elsewhere, and we in pursuit of the rest.

Thence, with my heart full of Joy, home, and to my office a little; then to my Lady Pen's, where they are all joyed and not a little puffed up at the good success of their father; and good service endeed is said to have been done by him. Had a great bonefire at the gate; and I with my Lady Pens people and others to Mrs Turner's great room, and then down into the street. I did give the boys 4s. among them – and mighty merry; so home to bed – with my heart at great rest and quiet, saving that the consideration of the victory is too great for me presently to comprehend.

10.   Lay long in bed; and then up and at the office all the morning. At noon dined at home, and then to the office, busy all the afternoon. In the evening home to supper, and there to my great trouble hear that the plague is come into the City (though it hath these three or four weeks since its beginning been wholly out of the City); but where should it begin but in my good friend and neighbour's, Dr Burnett in Fanchurch street – which in both points troubles me mightily.

11.   *Lords day.* Up, and expected long a new suit; but coming not, dressed myself in my late new black silk camelot suit; and when full ready, comes my new one of Colour'd Farrinden, which my wife puts me out of love with; which vexes [me], but I think it is only my not being used to wear Colours, which makes it look a little unusual upon me. To my chamber, and there spent the morning reading. At noon by invitation comes my two cousin Joyces and their wifes – my aunt James, and he-cousin Harman – his wife being ill. I had a good dinner for them, and as merry as I could be in such company. They being gone, I out of doors a little to show forsooth my new suit,

and back again; and in going, saw poor Dr Burnets door shut. But he hath, I hear, gained great goodwill among his neighbours; for he discovered it himself first, and caused himself to be shut up of his own accord – which was very handsome. In the evening comes Mr Andrews and his wife and Mr Hill, and stayed and played and sung and supped – most excellent pretty company; so pleasant, ingenious, and harmless, I cannot desire better. They gone, we to bed – my mind in great present ease.

13.   Up, and to the office, where all the morning doing business. At noon with Sir G. Carteret to my Lord Mayors to dinner, where much company in a little room – and though a good, yet no extraordinary Table. His name, Sir John Lawrence – whose father, a very ordinary old man, sat there at table – but it seems a very rich man. [Ald. Sir Richard Browne] did here openly tell in boasting, how he had, only upon suspicion of disturbances (if there had been any bad news from sea), clapped up several persons that he was afeared of. And that he had several times done the like and would do, and take no bail where he saw it unsafe for the King.

14.   I met with Mr Cowling, who observed to me how he finds everybody silent in the praise of my Lord of Sandwich, to set up the Duke and the Prince. But that the Duke did, both to the King and my Lord Chancellor, write abundantly of my Lord's courage and service. And

I this day met with a letter of Capt. Ferrers, where he tells us my Lord was with his ship in all the heat of the day, and did most worthily. Met with Creed, and he and I to Westminster and there saw my Lord Marlborough brought to be buried – several Lords of the Council carrying him, and with the Heralds in some state. Thence, vexed in my mind to think that I do so little in my Tanger business, and so home, and after supper to bed.

15. Up, and put on my new stuff suit with close knees, which becomes me most nobly as my wife says. At the office all day. At noon put on my first laced band, all lace, and to Kate Joyce's to dinner; where my mother, wife, and abundance of their friends, and good usage. Thence wife and Mercer and I to the Old Exchange and there bought two lace bands more, one of my Semstresse, whom my wife concurs with me to be a pretty woman. So down to Deptford and Woolwich, my boy and I. At Woolwich discoursed with Mr Shelden about my bringing my wife down for a month or two to his house; which he approves of, and I think will be very convenient. So late back and to the office, wrote letters, and so home to supper and to bed. This day the Newsbook (upon Mr Moores showing Lestrange Capt. Ferrers letter) did do my Lord Sandwich great right as to the late victory. The Duke of Yorke not yet come to town.

The town grows very sickly, and people to be afeared of it – there dying this last week of the plague 112, from

43 the week before – whereof, one in Fanchurch street and one in Broadstreete by the Treasurer's office.

16.   Up, and to the office, where I set hard to business – but was informed that the Duke of Yorke is come, and hath appointed us to attend him this afternoon. So after dinner and doing some business at the office, I to White-hall, where the Court is full of the Duke and his Courtiers, returned from sea – all fat and lusty, and ruddy by being in the sun. I kissed his hands, and we waited all the after-noon. By and by saw Mr Coventry, which rejoiced my very heart. Anon he and I from all the rest of the company walked into the matted gallery – where after many expres-sions of love, we fell to talk of business. Among other things, how my Lord Sandwich, both in his counsels and personal service, hath done most honorably and service-ably. Sir J. Lawson is come to Greenwich, but his wound in his knee yet very bad. Jonas Poole in the *Vantguard* did basely, so as to be, or will be, turned out of his ship. Capt. Holmes, expecting upon Sansums death to be made Rere-admirall to the Prince (but Harman is put in), hath delivered up to the Duke his commission, which the Duke took and tore. He, it seems, had bid the Prince, who first told him of Holmes's intention, that he should dissuade him from it, for that he was resolved to take it if he offered it. Yet Holmes would do it, like a rash, proud coxcomb – but he is rich, and hath it seems sought an occasion of leaving the service. Several of our Captains have done ill.

The great Shipps are the ships do the business, they quite deadening the enemy – they run away upon sight of the *Prince*. It is strange, to see how people do already slight Sir Wm. Berkely, my Lord Fitzharding's brother, who three months since was the delight of the Court. Capt. Smith of the *Mary*, the Duke talks mightily of, and some great thing will be done for him. Strange, to hear how the Dutch do relate, as the Duke says, that they are the conquerors – and bonefires are made in Dunkirke in their behalf – though a clearer victory can never be expected. Mr Coventry thinks they cannot have lost less then 6000 men; and we not dead above 200, and wounded about 400; in all, about 600. Thence home, and to my office till past 12 and then home to supper and to bed – my wife and mother not being yet come home from W. Hewres chamber, who treats my mother tonight. Capt. Grove, the Duke told us this day, hath done the basest thing at Lastoffe, in hearing of the guns and could not (as others) be got out, but stayed there – for which he will be tried; and is reckoned a prating coxcombe, and of no courage.

17.   It stroke me very deep this afternoon, going with a Hackny-coach from my Lord Treasurer's down Holborne – the coachman I found to drive easily and easily; at last stood still, and came down hardly able to stand; and told me that he was suddenly stroke very sick and almost blind, he could not see. So I light and went into another

coach, with a sad heart for the poor man and trouble for myself, lest he should have been stroke with the plague – being at that end of the town that I took him up. But God have mercy upon us all. Sir Jo. Lawson, I hear, is worse then yesterday – the King went to see him today, most kindly. It seems his wound is not very bad, but he hath a fever – a thrush and a Hickup, all three together; which are, it seems, very bad symptoms.

20. *Thanksgiving day for Victory over the Dutch.* Up, and to the office, where very busy alone all the morning till church time; and there heard a mean sorry sermon of Mr Mills. Then to the Dolphin Taverne, where all we officers of the Navy met with the Comissioners of the Ordnance by agreement and dined – where good Musique, at my direction. Our club came to 34s. a man – nine of us. Thence after dinner I to Whitehall with Sir W. Berkely in his coach. And so I walked to Herberts and there spent a little time avec la mosa, sin hazer algo con ella que kiss and tocar ses mamelles, que me haza hazer la cosa a mi mismo con gran plaisir. Thence by water to Foxhall, and there walked an hour alone, observing the several humours of the citizens that were there this holiday, pulling of cherries and God knows what. And so home to my office, where late, my wife not being come home with my mother, who have been this day all abroad upon the water, my mother being to go out of town speedily. So I home and to supper and to bed. This day I

informed myself that there died four or five at Westminster of the plague, in one alley in several houses upon Sunday last – Bell Alley, over against the Palace gate. Yet people do think that the number will be fewer in the town then it was the last week.

24. *Midsummer Day*. Up very betimes, by 6, and at Dr Clerkes at Westminster by 7 of the clock, having overnight by a note acquainted him with my intention of coming. And there I, in the best manner I could, broke my errand about a match between Sir G. Carterets eldest son and my Lord Sandwiches eldest daughter – which he (as I knew he would) took with great content; and we both agreed that my Lord and he, being both men relating to the sea – under a kind aspect of His Majesty – already good friends, and both virtuous and good families, their allyance might be of good use to us. And he did undertake to find out Sir George this morning, and put the business in execution. So being both well pleased with the proposition, I saw his neece there and made her sing me two or three songs, very prettily; and so home to the office – where to my great trouble, I found Mr Coventry and the board met before I came. I excused my late coming, by having been upon the River about office business. So to business all the morning. [After dinner] to Dr Clerke, and there find that he hath broke the business to Sir G. Carteret and that he takes the thing mighty well. Thence I to Sir G. Carteret at his Chamber, and in the

best manner I could, and most obligingly, moved that business; he received it with great respect and content and thanks to me, and promised that he would do what he could possibly for his son, to render him fit for my Lord's daughter. And showed great kindness to me, and sense of my kindness to him herein. Sir Wm. Pen told me this day that Mr Coventry is to be sworn a Privy Counsellor – at which my soul is glad. So home and to my letters by the post, and so home – to supper and bed.

25. *Lords day*. Up, and several people about business came to me by appointment, relating to the office; thence I to my closet about my Tanger papers. At noon dined. And then I abroad by water, it raining hard, thinking to have gone down to Woolwich; but I did not, but back through bridge to Whitehall – where after I had again visited Sir G. Carteret and received his (and now his Lady's) full content in my proposal, I went to my Lord Sandwich; and having told him how Sir G. Carteret received it, he did direct me to return to Sir G. Carteret and give him thanks for his kind reception of this offer, and that he would the next day be willing to enter discourse with him about that business. Which message I did presently do, and so left the business, with great joy to both sides. My Lord, I perceive, entends to give 5000*l* with her, and expects about 800*l* per annum joynture. So by water home and to supper and bed, being weary with

long walking at Court. But had a psalm or two with my boy and Mercer before bed, which pleased me mightily.

26.   The plague encreases mightily – I this day seeing a house, at a bittmakers over against St Clements church in the open street, shut up; which is a sad sight.

29.   Up, and by water to Whitehall, where the Court full of waggons and people ready to go out of town. The Mortality bill is come to 267 – which is about 90 more then the last; and of these, but 4 in the City – which is a great blessing to us. So home, calling at Somersett house, where all are packing up too; the Queene-mother setting out for France this day to drink Bourbon waters this year, she being in a consumption – and entends not to come till winter come twelvemonths. To the office, where busy a while, putting some things in my office in order, and then to letters till night. About 10 a-clock home – the days being sensibly shorter: before, I have once kept a summer's day by shutting up office by daylight, but my life hath been still as it was in winter almost. But I will for a month try what I can do by daylight. So home to supper and to bed.

30.   Thus this book of two years ends. Myself and family in good health, consisting of myself and wife – Mercer, her woman – Mary, Alice and Su, our maids; and Tom,

my boy. In a sickly time, of the plague growing on. Having upon my hands the troublesome care of the Treasury of Tanger, with great sums drawn upon me and nothing to pay them with. Also, the business of the office great. Consideration of removing my wife to Woolwich. She lately busy in learning to paint, with great pleasure and successe. All other things well; especially a new interest I am making, by a match in hand between the eldest son of Sir G. Carteret and my Lady Jemimah Mountagu. The Duke of York gone down to the fleet; but, all suppose, not with intent to stay there – as it is not fit, all men conceive, he should.[1]

1.   sc. as heir presumptive to the King.

September 1666

2. *Lords day*. Some of our maids sitting up late last night to get things ready against our feast today, Jane called us up, about 3 in the morning, to tell us of a great fire they saw in the City. So I rose, and slipped on my nightgown and went to her window, and thought it to be on the back side of Markelane at the furthest; but being unused to such fires as fallowed, I thought it far enough off, and so went to bed again and to sleep. About 7 rose again to dress myself, and there looked out at the window and saw the fire not so much as it was, and further off. So to my closet to set things to rights after yesterday's cleaning. By and by Jane comes and tells me that she hears that above 300 houses have been burned down tonight by the fire we saw, and that it was now burning down all Fishstreet by London Bridge. So I made myself ready presently, and walked to the Tower and there got up upon one of the high places, Sir J. Robinsons little son going up with me; and there I did see the houses at that end of the bridge all on fire, and an infinite great fire on this and the other side the end of the bridge – which, among other people,

did trouble me for poor little Michell and our Sarah on the Bridge. So down, with my heart full of trouble, to the Lieutenant of the Tower, who tells me that it begun this morning in the King's bakers house in Pudding lane, and that it hath burned down St Magnes Church and most part of Fishstreete already. So I down to the waterside and there got a boat and through the bridge, and there saw a lamentable fire. Poor Michells house, as far as the Old Swan, already burned that way and the fire running further, that in a very little time it got as far as the Still-yard while I was there. Everybody endeavouring to remove their goods, and flinging into the River or bring-ing them into lighters that lay off. Poor people staying in their houses as long as till the very fire touched them, and then running into boats or clambering from one pair of stair by the waterside to another. And among other things, the poor pigeons I perceive were loath to leave their houses, but hovered about the windows and balconies till they were some of them burned, their wings, and fell down.

Having stayed, and in an hour's time seen the fire rage every way, and nobody to my sight endeavouring to quench it, but to remove their goods and leave all to the fire; and having seen it get as far as the Steeleyard, and the wind mighty high and driving it into the city, and everything, after so long a drougth, proving combustible, even the very stones of churches, and among other things, the poor steeple by which pretty Mrs [Horsley] lives, and

whereof my old schoolfellow Elborough is parson, taken
fire in the very top and there burned till it fall down – I
to Whitehall with a gentleman with me who desired to
go off from the Tower to see the fire in my boat – to
Whitehall, and there up to the King's closet in the chapel,
where people came about me and I did give them an
account dismayed them all; and word was carried in to
the King, so I was called for and did tell the King and
Duke of York what I saw, and that unless his Majesty did
command houses to be pulled down, nothing could stop
the fire. They seemed much troubled, and the King commanded me to go to my Lord Mayor from him and
command him to spare no houses but to pull down before
the fire every way. The Duke of York bid me tell him that
if he would have any more soldiers, he shall; and so did
my Lord Arlington afterward, as a great secret. Here meet-
ing with Capt. Cocke, I in his coach, which he lent me,
and Creed with me, to Pauls; and there walked along
Watling street as well as I could, every creature coming
away loaden with goods to save – and here and there sick
people carried away in beds. Extraordinary good goods
carried in carts and on backs. At last met my Lord Mayor
in Canning Streete, like a man spent, with a handkercher
about his neck. To the King's message, he cried like a
fainting woman, 'Lord, what can I do? I am spent! People
will not obey me. I have been pull[ing] down houses. But
the fire overtakes us faster then we can do it.' That he
needed no more soldiers; and that for himself, he must

go and refresh himself, having been up all night. So he left me, and I him, and walked home – seeing people all almost distracted and no manner of means used to quench the fire. The houses too, so very thick thereabouts, and full of matter for burning, as pitch and tar, in Thames street – and warehouses of oyle and wines and Brandy and other things. Here I saw Mr Isaccke Houblon, that handsome man – prettily dressed and dirty at his door at Dowgate, receiving some of his brothers things whose houses were on fire; and as he says, have been removed twice already, and he doubts (as it soon proved) that they must be in a little time removed from his house also – which was a sad consideration. And to see the churches all filling with goods, by people who themselfs should have been quietly there at this time. By this time it was about 12 a-clock, and so home and there find my guests, which was Mr Wood and his wife, Barbary Shelden, and also Mr Moone – she mighty fine, and her husband, for aught I see, a likely man. But Mr Moones design and mine, which was to look over my closet and please him with the sight thereof, which he hath long desired, was wholly disappointed, for we were in great trouble and disturbance at this fire, not knowing what to think of it. However, we had an extraordinary good dinner, and as merry as at this time we could be. While at dinner, Mrs Batelier came to enquire after Mr Woolfe and Stanes (who it seems are related to them), whose houses in

Fishstreet are all burned, and they in a sad condition. She would not stay in the fright.

As soon as dined, I and Moone away and walked through the City, the streets full of nothing but people and horses and carts loaden with goods, ready to run over one another, and removing goods from one burned house to another – they now removing out of Canning street (which received goods in the morning) into Lumbard Streete and further; and among others, I now saw my little goldsmith Stokes receiving some friend's goods, whose house itself was burned the day after. We parted at Pauls, he home and I to Pauls Wharf, where I had appointed a boat to attend me; and took in Mr Carcasse and his brother, whom I met in the street, and carried them below and above bridge, to and again, to see the fire, which was now got further, both below and above, and no likelihood of stopping it. Met with the King and Duke of York in their Barge, and with them to Queen Hith and there called Sir Rd. Browne to them. Their order was only to pull down houses apace, and so below bridge at the waterside; but little was or could be done, the fire coming upon them so fast. Good hopes there was of stopping it at the Three Cranes above, and at Buttolphs Wharf below bridge, if care be used; but the wind carries it into the City, so as we know not by the waterside what it doth there. River full of lighter[s] and boats taking in goods, and good goods swimming in the water; and only,

I observed that hardly one lighter or boat in three that had goods of a house in, but there was a pair of virginalls in it. Having seen as much as I could now, I away to Whitehall by appointment, and there walked to St James's Park, and there met my wife and Creed and Wood and his wife and walked to my boat, and there upon the water again, and to the fire up and down, it still increasing and the wind great. So near the fire as we could for smoke; and all over the Thames, with one's face in the wind you were almost burned with a shower of Firedrops – this is very true – so as houses were burned by these drops and flakes of fire, three or four, nay five or six houses, one from another. When we could endure no more upon the water, we to a little alehouse on the Bankside over against the Three Cranes, and there stayed till it was dark almost and saw the fire grow; and as it grow darker, appeared more and more, and in Corners and upon steeples and between churches and houses, as far as we could see up the hill of the City, in a most horrid malicious bloody flame, not like the fine flame of an ordinary fire. Barbary and her husband away before us. We stayed till, it being darkish, we saw the fire as only one entire arch of fire from this to the other side of the bridge, and in a bow up the hill, for an arch of above a mile long. It made me weep to see it. The churches, houses, and all on fire and flaming at once, and a horrid noise the flames made, and the cracking of houses at their ruine.

So home with a sad heart, and there find everybody

discoursing and lamenting the fire; and poor Tom Hater came with some few of his goods saved out of his house, which is burned upon Fish street hill. I invited him to lie at my house, and did receive his goods: but was deceived in his lying there, the noise coming every moment of the growth of the Fire, so as we were forced to begin to pack up our own goods and prepare for their removal. And did by Mooneshine (it being brave, dry, and moonshine and warm weather) carry much of my goods into the garden, and Mr Hater and I did remove my money and Iron chests into my cellar – as thinking that the safest place. And got my bags of gold into my office ready to carry away, and my chief papers of accounts also there, and my tallies into a box by themselfs. So great was our fear, as Sir W. Batten had carts come out of the country to fetch away his goods this night. We did put Mr Hater, poor man, to bed a little; but he got but very little rest, so much noise being in my house, taking down of goods.

3.   About 4 a-clock in the morning, my Lady Batten sent me a cart to carry away all my money and plate and best things to Sir W. Riders at Bednall greene; which I did, riding myself in my nightgown in the Cart; and Lord, to see how the streets and the highways are crowded with people, running and riding and getting of carts at any rate to fetch away thing[s]. I find Sir W. Rider tired with being called up all night and receiving things from several friends. His house full of goods – and much of Sir W.

Batten and Sir W. Penn's. I am eased at my heart to have my treasure so well secured. Then home with much ado to find a way. Nor any sleep all this night to me nor my poor wife. But then, and all this day, she and I and all my people labouring to get away the rest of our things, and did get Mr Tooker to get me a lighter to take them in, and we did carry them (myself some) over Tower hill, which was by this time full of people's goods, bringing their goods thither. And down to the lighter, which lay at the next quay above the Tower dock. And there was my neighbour's wife, Mrs [Buckworth], with her pretty child and some few of her things, which I did willingly give way to be saved with mine. But there was no passing with anything through the postern, the crowd was so great. The Duke of York came this day by the office and spoke to us, and did ride with his guard up and down the City to keep all quiet (he being now General, and having the care of all). This day, Mercer being not at home, but against her mistress order gone to her mother's, and my wife going thither to speak with W. Hewer, met her there and was angry; and her mother saying that she was not a prentice girl, to ask leave every time she goes abroad, my wife with good reason was angry, and when she came home, bid her be gone again. And so she went away, which troubled me; but yet less then it would, because of the condition we are in fear of coming into in a little time, of being less able to keep one in her quality. At night, lay down a little upon a quilt of W. Hewer in the office (all my own things being packed up or gone); and after me, my poor wife did the like – we having fed upon the remains of yesterday's dinner, having no fire nor dishes, nor any opportunity of dressing anything.

4.   Up by break of day to get away the remainder of my things, which I did by a lighter at the Iron gate; and my hands so few, that it was the afternoon before we could get them all away. Sir W. Penn and I to Tower street, and there met the fire Burning three or four doors beyond Mr Howells; whose goods, poor man (his trayes and dishes, Shovells &c., were flung all along Tower street in the kennels, and people working therewith from one end to the other), the fire coming on in that narrow street, on both sides, with infinite fury. Sir W. Batten, not knowing how to remove his wind, did dig a pit in the garden and laid it in there; and I took the opportunity of laying all the papers of my office that I could not otherwise dispose of. And in the evening Sir W. Penn and I did dig another and put our wine in it, and I my parmazan cheese as well as my wine and some other things. The Duke of York was at the office this day at Sir W. Penn's, but I happened not to be within. This afternoon, sitting melancholy with Sir W. Penn in our garden and thinking of the certain burning of this office without extraordinary means, I did propose for the sending up of all our workmen from Woolwich and Deptford yards (none whereof yet appeared), and to write to Sir W. Coventry to have the

Duke of York's permission to pull down houses rather then lose this office, which would much hinder the King's business. So Sir W. Penn he went down this night, in order to the sending them up tomorrow morning; and I wrote to Sir W. Coventry about the business, but received no answer.

This night Mrs Turner (who, poor woman, was removing her goods all this day – good goods, into the garden, and knew not how to dispose of them) – and her husband supped with my wife and I at night in the office, upon a shoulder of mutton from the cook's, without any napkin or anything, in a sad manner but were merry. Only, now and then walking into the garden and saw how horridly the sky looks, all on a fire in the night, was enough to put us out of our wits; and endeed it was extremely dreadfull – for it looks just as if it was at us, and the whole heaven on fire. I after supper walked in the dark down to Tower street, and there saw it all on fire at the Trinity house on that side and the Dolphin tavern on this side, which was very near us – and the fire with extraordinary vehemence. Now begins the practice of blowing up of houses in Tower street, those next the Tower, which at first did frighten people more then anything; but it stop[ped] the fire where it was done – it bringing down the houses to the ground in the same places they stood, and then it was easy to quench what little fire was in it, though it kindled nothing almost. W. Hewer this day went to see how his mother did, and comes late home, but telling us how he hath been forced to remove her to Islington, her house in Pye Corner being burned. So that it is got so far that way and all the Old Bayly, and was running down to Fleet street. And Pauls is burned, and all Cheapside. I wrote to my father this night; but the post-house being burned, the letter could not go.

5.   I lay down in the office again upon W. Hewer's quilt, being mighty weary and sore in my feet with going till I was hardly able to stand. About 2 in the morning my wife calls me up and tells of new Cryes of 'Fyre!' – it being come to Barkeing Church, which is the bottom of our lane. I up; and finding it so, resolved presently to take her away; and did, and took my gold (which was about 23 50*l*), W. Hewer, and Jane down by Poundy's boat to Woolwich. But Lord, what a sad sight it was by moonlight to see the whole City almost on fire – that you might see it plain at Woolwich, as if you were by it. There when I came, I find the gates shut, but no guard kept at all; which troubled me, because of discourses now begun that there is plot in it and that the French had done it. I got the gates open, and to Mr Shelden's, where I locked up my gold and charged my wife and W. Hewer never to leave the room without one of them in it night nor day. So back again, by the way seeing my goods well in the lighters at Deptford and watched well by people. Home, and whereas I expected to have seen our house on fire, it being now about 7 a-clock, it was not. But to the Fyre, and there

find greater hopes then I expected; for my confidence of finding our office on fire was such, that I durst not ask anybody how it was with us, till I came and saw it not burned. But going to the fire, I find, by the blowing up of houses and the great help given by the workmen out of the King's yards, sent up by Sir W. Penn, there is a good stop given to it, as well at Marke lane end as ours – it having only burned the Dyall of Barkeing Church, and part of the porch, and was there quenched. I up to the top of Barkeing steeple, and there saw the saddest sight of desolation that I ever saw. Everywhere great fires. Oyle cellars and brimstone and other things burning. I became afeared to stay there long; and therefore down again as fast as I could, the fire being spread as far as I could see it, and to Sir W. Penn's and there eat a piece of cold meat, having eaten nothing since Sunday but the remains of Sunday's dinner.

Here I met with Mr Young and Whistler; and having removed all my things, and received good hopes that the fire at our end is stopped, they and I walked into the town and find Fanchurch street, Gracious street, and Lumbard street all in dust. The Exchange a sad sight, nothing standing there of all the statues or pillars but Sir Tho. Gresham's picture in the corner. Walked into Moorefields (our feet ready to burn, walking through the town among the hot coles) and find that full of people, and poor wretches carrying their goods there, and everybody keeping his goods together by themselfs (and a great blessing it is to them that it is fair weather for them to keep abroad night and day); drank there, and paid twopence for a plain penny loaf. Thence homeward, having passed through Cheapside and Newgate market, all burned – and seen Anthony Joyces house in fire. And took up (which I keep by me) a piece of glass of Mercer's chapel in the street, where much more was, so melted and buckled with the heat of the fire, like parchment. I also did see a poor Catt taken out of a hole in the chimney joyning to the wall of the Exchange, with the hair all burned off the body and yet alive. So home at night, and find there good hopes of saving our office – but great endeavours of watching all night and having men ready; and so we lodged them in the office, and had drink and bread and cheese for them. And I lay down and slept a good night about midnight – though when I rose, I hear that there had been a great alarme of French and Duch being risen – which proved nothing. But it is a strange thing to see how long this time did look since Sunday, having been alway full of variety of actions, and little sleep, that it looked like a week or more. And I had forgot almost the day of the week.

6. Up about 5 a-clock, and there met Mr Gawden at the gate of the office (I entending to go out, as I used every now and then to do, to see how the fire is) to call our men to Bishoppsgate, where no fire had yet been near, and there is now one broke out – which did give great grounds

to people, and to me too, to think that there is some kind of plott in this (on which many by this time have been taken, and it hath been dangerous for any stranger to walk in the streets); but I went with the men and we did put it out in a little time, so that that was well again. It was pretty to see how hard the women did work in the cannells sweeping of water; but then they would scold for drink and be as drunk as devils. I saw good Butts of sugar broke open in the street, and people go and take handfuls out and put into beer and drink it. And now all being pretty well, I took boat and over to Southwarke, and took boat on the other side the bridge and so to Westminster, thinking to Shift myself, being all in dirt from top to bottom. But could not there find any place to buy a Shirt or pair of gloves, Westminster hall being full of people's goods – those in Westminster having removed all their goods, and the Exchequer money put into vessels to carry to Nonsuch. But to the Swan, and there was trimmed. And then to Whitehall, but saw nobody, and so home. A sad sight to see how the River looks – no houses nor church near it to the Temple – where it stopped. At home did go with Sir W. Batten and our neighbour Knightly (who, with one more, was the only man of any fashion left in all the neighbourhood hereabouts, they all removing their goods and leaving their houses to the mercy of the fire) to Sir R. Ford's, and there dined, in an earthen platter a fried breast of mutton, a great many of us. But very merry; and endeed as good a meal, though as ugly a one, as ever I had in my life. Thence down to Deptford, and there with great satisfaction landed all my goods at Sir G. Carteret's, safe, and nothing missed I could see, or hurt. This being done to my great content, I home; and to Sir W. Batten's and there with Sir R. Ford, Mr Knightly, and one Withers, a professed lying rogue, supped well; and mighty merry and our fears over. From them to the office and there slept, with the office full of labourers, who talked and slept and walked all night long there. But strange it was to see Cloathworkers hall on fire these three days and nights in one body of Flame – it being the cellar, full of Oyle.

7.   Up by 5 a-clock and, blessed be God, find all well, and by water to Paul's wharfe. Walked thence and saw all the town burned, and a miserable sight of Pauls church, with all the roofs fallen and the body of the Quire fallen into St Fayths – Paul's school also – Ludgate – Fleet street – my father's house, and the church, and a good part of the Temple the like. So to Creeds lodging near the New Exchange, and there find him laid down upon a bed – the house all unfurnished, there being fears of the fire's coming to them. There borrowed a shirt of him – and washed. To Sir W. Coventry at St James's, who lay without Curtains, having removed all his goods – as the King at Whitehall and everybody had done and was doing. He hopes we shall have no public distractions upon this fire, which is what everybody fears – because of the talk of

the French having a hand in it. And it is a proper time for discontents – but all men's minds are full of care to protect themselfs and save their goods. The Militia is in armes everywhere. Our fleetes, he tells me, have been in sight of one another, and most unhappily by Fowle weather were parted, to our great loss, as in reason they do conclude – the Duch being come out only to make a show and please their people; but in very bad condition as to stores, victuals, and men. They are at Bullen, and our fleet come to St Ellens. We have got nothing, but have lost one ship, but he knows not what.

Thence to the Swan and there drank; and so home and find all well. My Lord Brouncker at Sir W. Batten's, and tells us the Generall is sent for up to come to advise with the King about business at this juncture, and to keep all quiet – which is great honour to him, but I am sure is but a piece of dissimulation. So home and did give order for my house to be made clean; and then down to Woolwich and there find all well. Dined, and Mrs Markeham came to see my wife. So I up again, and calling at Deptford for some things of W. Hewer, he being with me; and then home and spent the evening with Sir R. Ford, Mr Knightly, and Sir W. Penn at Sir W. Batten's. This day our Merchants first met at Gresham College, which by proclamation is to be their Exchange. Strange to hear what is bid for houses all up and down here – a friend of Sir W. Riders having 150*l* for what he used to let for 40*l* per annum. Much dispute where the Custome house shall be; thereby the growth of the City again to be foreseen. My Lord Treasurer, they say, and others, would have it at the other end of the town. I home late to Sir W. Penn, who did give me a bed – but without curtains or hangings, all being down. So here I went the first time into a naked bed, only my drawers on – and did sleep pretty well; but still, both sleeping and waking, had a fear of fire in my heart, that I took little rest. People do all the world over cry out of the simplicity of my Lord Mayor in general, and more perticularly in this business of the fire, laying it all upon him. A proclamation is come out for markets to be kept at Leadenhall and Mile end greene and several other places about the town, and Tower hill, and all churches to be set open to receive poor people.

8.　Up, and with Sir W. Batten and Sir W. Penn by water to Whitehall, and they to St James's. I stopped with Sir G. Carteret, to desire him to go with us and to enquire after money. But the first he cannot do, and the other as little, or says, 'When can we get any, or what shall we do for it?' He, it seems, is imployed in the correspondence between the City and the King every day, in settling of things. I find him full of trouble to think how things will go. I left him, and to St James's, where we met first at Sir W. Coventry's chamber and there did what business we can without any books. Our discourse, as everything else, was confused. The fleet is at Portsmouth, there staying a wind to carry them to the Downes or toward Bullen, where they say the Duch fleete is gone and stays. We concluded upon private meetings for a while, not having any money to satisfy any people that may come to us. I bought two eeles upon the Thames, cost me 6*s*. Thence with Sir W. Batten to the Cockpit, whither the Duke of Albemarle is come. It seems the King holds him so necessary at this time, that he hath sent for him and will keep him here. Endeed, his interest in the City, being acquainted, and his care in keeping things quiet, is reckoned that wherein he will be very serviceable. We to him. He is courted in appearance by everybody. He very kind to us. I perceive he lays by all business of the fleet at present and minds the City, and is now hastening to Gresham College to discourse with the Aldermen. Sir W. Batten and I home (where met by my Brother John, come to town to see how things are with us). And then presently he with me to Gresham College – where infinite of people; partly through novelty to see the new place, and partly to find out and hear what is become one man of another. I met with many people undone, and more that have extraordinary great losses. People speaking their thoughts variously about the beginning of the fire and the rebuilding of the City. Then to Sir W. Batten and took my brother with me, and there dined with a great company of neighbours, and much good discourse; among others, of the low spirits of some rich men in the City, in sparing any encouragement to the poor people that wrought for the saving their houses. Among others, Ald. Starling, a very rich man, without children, the fire at next door to him in our Lane – after our men had saved his house, did give 2*s*. 6*d*. among 30 of them, and did quarrel with some that would remove the rubbish out of the way of the fire, saying that they came to steal. Sir. W. Coventry told me of another this morning in Holborne, which he showed the King – that when it was offered to stop the fire near his house for such a reward, that came but to 2*s*. 6*d*. a man among the neighbours, he would give but 18*d*. Thence to Bednall green by coach, my brother with me, and saw all well there and fetched away my Journall-book to enter for five days past. To the office, and late writing letters; and then to Sir W. Penn, my brother lying with me, and Sir W. Penn gone down to rest himself at Woolwich. But I was much frighted, and kept awake in my bed, by some noise I heard a great while below-stairs and the boys not coming up to me when I knocked. It was by their discovery of people stealing of some neighbours' wine that lay in vessels in the street. So to sleep. And all well all night.

9.   *Sunday*. Up, and was trimmed, and sent my brother to Woolwich to my wife to dine with her. I to church, where our parson made a melancholy but good sermon – and many, and most, in the church cried, especially the women. The church mighty full, but few of fashion, and most strangers. I walked to Bednall green; and there dined well, but a bad venison pasty, at Sir W. Rider's.

Good people they are, and good discourse. And his daughter Middleton, a fine woman and discreet. Thence home, and to church again, and there preached Deane Harding; but methinks a bad poor sermon, though proper for the time – nor eloquent, in saying at this time that the City is reduced from a large Folio to a Decimo tertio. So to my office, there to write down my journall and take leave of my brother, whom I sent back this afternoon, though rainy – which it hath not done a good while before. But I had no room nor convenience for him here till my house is fitted; but I was very kind to him, and do take very well of him his journey. I did give him 40s. for his pocket; and so he being gone, and it presently rayning, I was troubled for him, though it is good for the Fyre. Anon to Sir W. Penn to bed, and made my boy Tom to read me asleep.

13. Up, and down to Tower wharfe; and there with Balty and labourers from Deptford did get my goods housed well at home. So down to Deptford again to fetch the rest, and there eat a bit of dinner at the Globe, with the maister of the *Bezan* with me, while the labourers went to dinner. Here I hear that this poor town doth bury still of the plague seven or eight in a day. So to Sir G. Carteret's to work; and there did, to my great content, ship off into the *Bezan* all the rest of my goods, saving my pictures and fine things, that I will bring home in wherrys when my house is fit to receive them. And so home and unloaden

them by carts and hands before night, to my exceeding
satisfaction; and so after supper to bed in my house, the
first time I have lain there; and lay with my wife in my
old closet upon the ground, and Balty and his wife in the
best chamber, upon the ground also.

14. Up, and to work, having Carpenters come to help
in setting up bedsteads and hangings; and at that trade
my people and I all the morning, till pressed by public
business to leave them, against my will, in the afternoon;
and yet I was troubled in being at home, to see all my
goods lie up and down the house in a bad condition, and
strange workmen going to and fro might take what they
would almost. All the afternoon busy; and Sir W. Coventry came to me, and found me, as God would have it, in
my office, and people about me setting my papers to
rights; and there discoursed about getting an account
ready against the Parliament, and thereby did create me
infinite of business, and to be done on a sudden, which
troubled me; but however, he being gone, I about it late
to good purpose; and so home, having this day also got
my wine out of the ground again and set it in my cellar;
but with great pain to keep the port[er]s that carried it
in from observing the money-chests there. So to bed as
last night; only, my wife and I upon a bedstead with
curtains in that which was Mercer's chamber, and Balty
and his wife (who are here and do us good service) where
we lay last night.

15. All morning at the office, Harman being come, to my great satisfaction, to put up my beds and hangings; so I am at rest, and fallowed my business all day. Dined with Sir W. Batten. Mighty busy about this account, and while my people were busy, myself wrote near 30 letters and orders with my own hand. At it till 11 at night; and it is strange to see how clear my head was, being eased of all the matter of all those letters; whereas one would think that I should have been dozed – I never did observe so much of myself in my life. In the evening there comes to me Capt. Cocke, and walked a good while in the garden; he says he hath computed that the rents of houses lost this fire in the City comes to 600000*l* per annum. That this will make the Parliament more quiet then otherwise they would have been and give the King a more ready supply. That the supply must be by excise, as it is in holland. That the Parliament will see it necessary to carry on the war. That the late storm hindered our beating the Duch fleet, who were gone out only to satisfy the people, having no business to do but to avoid us. That the French, as late in the year as it is, are coming. That the Duch are really in bad condition, but that this unhappiness of ours doth give them heart. That, certainly, never so great a loss as this was borne so well by citizens in the world as this; he believing that not one merchant upon the Change will break upon it. That he doth not apprehend there will be any disturbances in estate upon it, for that all men are busy in looking after their own business, to save

themselfs. He gone, I to finish my letters; and home to bed and find, to my infinite joy, many rooms clean, and myself and wife lie in our own chamber again. But much terrified in the nights nowadays with dreams of fire and falling down of houses.